BRITISH-AMERICAN SYNONYMS

french fries and chips and other
WORDS THAT MEAN THE SAME THING
but look and sound as different as truck and lorry

BRITISH-AMERICAN SYNONYMS

ARTWORK BY JOAN HANSON

Published by
Lerner Publications Company
Minneapolis, Minnesota

For
Jenny, Doug,
Troy and Heather

International Standard Book Number: 0-8225-0279-8
Library of Congress Catalog Card Number: 72-3971

Third Printing 1974

syn·o·nym (SIN-uh-nim) A word that has the same or nearly the same meaning as another word. These words are synonyms: *little* and *small*; *big* and *large*; *pretty* and *attractive*.

Each pair of synonyms in this book consists of two names for the same thing. One name is generally used in the United States, the other in Great Britain.

Television

Telly

Line Up

Queue Up

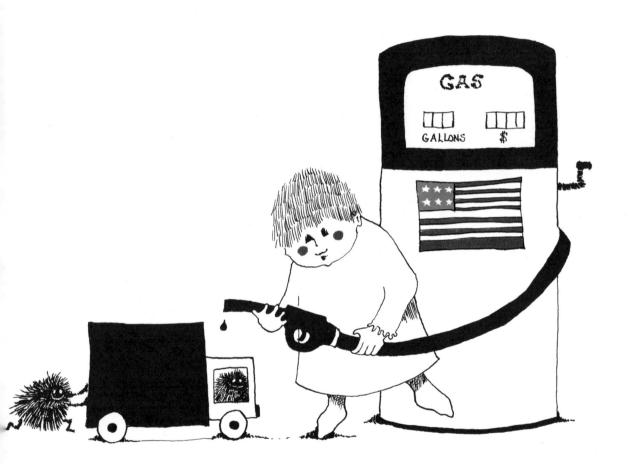

Gas

Petrol

Flashlight

Torch

KEEP
AMERICA
CLEAN!

Garbage Can

Dust Bin

Sidewalk

Pavement

French Fries

Chips

Diaper

Nappie

Napkin

Serviette

Elevator

Lift

Truck

Lorry

Candy Store

Sweet Shop

Can

Tin

BOOKS IN THIS SERIES

ANTONYMS
hot and cold and other
WORDS THAT ARE DIFFERENT
as night and day

MORE ANTONYMS
wild and tame and other
WORDS THAT ARE AS DIFFERENT IN MEANING
as work and play

HOMONYMS
hair and hare and other
WORDS THAT SOUND THE SAME
but look as different as bear and bare

MORE HOMONYMS
steak and stake and other
WORDS THAT SOUND THE SAME
but look as different as chili and chilly

HOMOGRAPHS
bow and bow and other
WORDS THAT LOOK THE SAME
but sound as different as sow and sow

HOMOGRAPHIC HOMOPHONES
fly and fly and other
WORDS THAT LOOK AND SOUND THE SAME
but are as different in meaning as bat and bat

British-American SYNONYMS
french fries and chips and other
WORDS THAT MEAN THE SAME THING
but look and sound
as different as truck and lorry

MORE SYNONYMS
shout and yell and other
WORDS THAT MEAN THE SAME THING
but look and sound
as different as loud and noisy

*We specialize in producing quality books for
young people. For a complete list please write*

LERNER PUBLICATIONS COMPANY
241 First Avenue North, Minneapolis, Minnesota 55401